love
Wendy

Dogtionary

Dogtionary

meaningful portraits
of dogs
by Sharon Montrose

VIKING STUDIO

VIKING STUDIO
Published by the Penguin Group
Penguin Putnam Inc., 375 Hudson Street, New York, New York 10014, U.S.A.
Penguin Books Ltd, 27 Wrights Lane, London W8 5TZ, England
Penguin Books Australia Ltd, Ringwood, Victoria, Australia
Penguin Books Canada Ltd, 10 Alcorn Avenue, Toronto, Ontario, Canada M4V 3B2
Penguin Books (N.Z.) Ltd, 182-190 Wairau Road, Auckland 10, New Zealand

Penguin Books Ltd, Registered Offices:
Harmondsworth, Middlesex, England

First published in 2001 by Viking Studio,
a member of Penguin Putnam Inc.

10 9 8 7 6 5 4 3

Copyright © Sharon Montrose, 2001
All rights reserved

CIP data available

ISBN 0-670-03499-1

This book is printed on acid-free paper. ∞

Printed in Japan

Set in Gobbler
Designed by Sharon Montrose

For Mom

PRONUNCIATION KEY

ə
- a in regal
- e in shepherd
- i in agile
- o in gallop
- u in zealous

a   wag, scratch
ā   trainer, stay
ä   bark, guard

b   ball, biscuit

ch   chow, catch

d   dig, bad

e   beg, pet
ē   flea, breed

f   fetch, sniff

g   greet, tag

h   heel, happy

i   lick, kiss
ī   climb, hide

j   jump, joy

k   kibble, tick

l   lap, cuddle

m   mastiff, groom

n   nap, bone
ŋ   tongue, drink

ō   obey, protect
ô   paw, snore

oo   curious, good
o͞o   drool, chew

oi   loyal, joyful
ou   growl, howl

p   play, sleep

r   retrieve, collar

s   sit, chase
sh   shake, leash

t   tail, treat
th   thief, filthy

u   run, gulp
ur   burrow, hurdle

v   vet, love

w   whisker, watch

y   yard, yawn

z   zonked, lazy

AMIGO

(ɵ mē´gō) n.

1. a buddy

2. a pal

3. a comrade

AVERY

(ā´ve rē)n.

1. Part Italian Greyhound   2. Part English Bulldog

3. ALL LOVE

BENNY (ben´ē)n.   1. Two Eyes   2. Four Legs   3. Thirty-Nine Wrinkles

BOOGIEMAN

(bʊʊg′ē man′)n.

1. a thirty-pound bodyguard

2. a four-legged security system

3. ACCEPTS BRIBES

BOSLEY

(bäs´lē)n.

1. needs food

2. needs water

3. NEEDS A HAIRCUT

CECIL

(sē´sool)n.

1. house for rent   2. big yard

3. NO CATS!!!

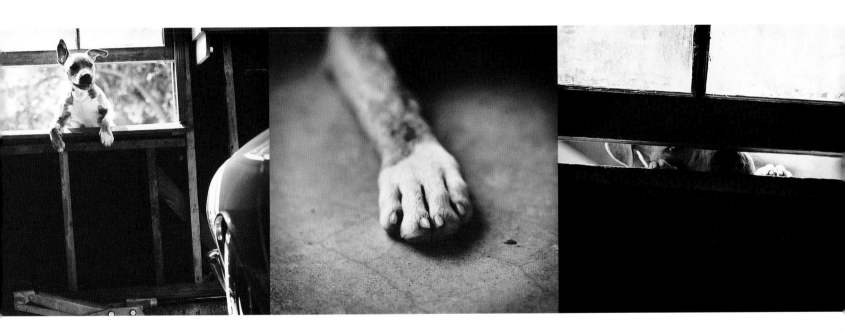

CRUMB

(krum)n.

1. a 5AM alarm clock

2. a 6AM alarm clock

3. a REASON to get up in the morning

DAISY

(dā´zē)n.

1. sniffs dry food

2. nibbles canned food

3. FEASTS on GRASS

DEXTER

(deks´ ter)n.

1. beautiful

2. insightful

3. respectful

DOLLY

(dal´-ē)n.

1. HATES plane rides   2. LIKES car rides

3. LOVES bike rides

DUSTY

(dus´tē)n.

1. pulls up the weeds

2. digs up the flowers

3. plants HERSELF in the dirt

ELKE

(el'kē)n.

1. watcher

2. observer

3. spectator

EMMA

(em′ ǝ)n.

1. hides from the vacuum cleaner

2. runs from the coffee grinder

3. CHASES GERMAN SHEPHERDS

FABLE

(fā´ bel)n.

1. Mirror

2. Mirror

3. On the wall

FLOYD

(flóid) n.

1. Jumps for Treats   2. Jumps for Frisbees

3. JUMPS for JOY!!!

FOREST (fôr´ist)n. 1. On your mark...   2. Get set...   3. GO!!!

GIDGET

(gĭj´ĭt)n.

1. he loves me

2. he loves me not

3. he loves me

HARRY

(har´ē)n.

1. shaggy

2. furry

3. fluffy

INDIGO

(inˊdi gōˊ)n.

1. will sit for a treat

2. will roll over for a biscuit

3. will do ANYTHING for a walk

JERSEY

(jer´-zē)n.

1. dog shy

2. people shy

3. camera shy

KISMET

(kiz´met)n.

1. meant 2. to 3. be

LUCY

(lōō′sē)n.

1. sandpaper tongue

2. ice cube nose

3. velvet ears

MISTER NELSON
(mist´er nels´en)n.

1. Gotta

2. Go

3. Potty

MURDOCH

(mʊr´däk)n.

1. grumpy

2. old

3. man

MUSKETEERS

(mus´ke tirs)n.

1. Athos

2. Porthos

3. Aramis

NASH

(nash)n.

1. Tic

2. Tac

3. TOE

NEAPOLITAN

(nē´ ə päl´ ə t'n)n.

1. Chocolate

2. Vanilla

3. Strawberry

NED

(ned)n.

1. steals the contractor's lunch

2. approves the final tile color

3. TESTS OUT THE NEW TOILET

OPHELIA

(ō fil´ē ɵ)n.

1. morning swims

2. sun-drenched naps

3. chilled water bowls

OTIS

(ōt´is)n.

1. Giant Snout

2. Giant Bark

3. Giant Heart

PEANUT

(pē´nut´)n.

1. greeting committee

2. seat warmer

3. party crasher

QUINCY

(kwin´sē)n.

1. drools on the couch

2. snores on the floor

3. dreams under the table

RAIF
(rāf)n.

1. never allowed on the sofa

2. sometimes allowed on the sofa

3. always allowed on the sofa

RITA

(rēt´ɘ)n.

1. signed   2. sealed   3. delivered

SAM (sam) n.   1. HATES $6 squeaky toy   2. IGNORES $3 chew bone   3. LOVES $75 running shoes

SIMON

(sīm´ un)n.

1. says: throw the ball!

2. says: throw the ball!

3. says: throw the ball!

SUNNY

(sun´ē)n.

1. Left

2. Right

3. Left, Right, Left

TITAN

(tīt´'n)n.

1. BEWARE

2. OF

3. TONGUE

UFO

(yoo′ef′ō)n.

1. Unidentified

2. Flying

3. Object

VADER

(vād´ ər)n.

1. clipped

2. filed

3. polished

VINNEY

(vin´ē)n.

1. found at the crime scene

2. covered with dirt

3. "NOT GUILTY"

WINSTON

(wins´tun)n.

1. Best of breed

2. Best in show

3. Doesn't do interviews

XENA

(zēn´ ɵ)n.

1. Canine   2. Princess   3. Warrior

YIN & YANG

(yin,yän)n.

1. indispensable

2. indivisible 3. inseparable

ZIGGY

(zig´ ē)n.

1. He came 2. He saw 3. He conquered

ACKNOWLEDGMENTS

I am extremely grateful to the following people who have in one way or another contributed to this book:

My mom, Doris Wise Montrose, for your love and support in my struggle to pursue my passion, and my brother, David Montrose, for your warm friendship and being the only person in the world who might know what it feels like to be me. I love you both endlessly.

My grandmother Fela Wise, for believing in me.
My grandfather Meyer Wise, who I know would have been very proud to see this book.

Dad and Annie, my grandmother Marian Montrose, and my very missed grandfather, Harry Montrose.

Carisha Zweigel, Jenny Hope, Jean Bourget, Ina Burke, Jackie Lee, Nancy Martin, Sally Field, Arnold Rubinoff, Larry Jones, Ford Lowcock, all the owners of the dogs photographed for this book, and special thanks to Bob Weinberg.

Joseph Viles, for being so generous with your knowledge. I will be forever grateful.

My second family at Photo Center: Vicki Berndt, Myk Mishoe, Deborah Hillman, Camilla Bratt, and Tembi Locke. Also Mikel Healey, for being a beautiful person and an incredible talent, and very special thanks to Craig Kovacs, for your immense loyalty and everything you have done for me over the years.

Special thanks to my editor, Christopher Sweet; also Michelle Li and the whole staff at Viking Studio.

I owe a huge debt of gratitude to my literary agent, Betsy Amster. Thank you.

And to the amazing creatures this book celebrates, I cannot imagine life without them.